MW01002243

Riverside's Street Names

The Stories Behind the Names of Riverside California's Major (and Some Minor) Streets

Steve Lech

Layout and Graphics:
Steve Lech

Cover Art:
Steve Lech

Published by the author

Table of Contents

Foreword

This book has been in the making for quite some time. I've collected various street names over the years, but never really did anything with it until now. I've always been fascinated with the names of places, streets, buildings, parks, etc., so it seems natural that a small volume like this one should be written.

That said, the reader of this must understand one thing. Unlike most historical research I've done which is documented in one or more ways, the names of streets are definitely not. No one in Riverside's past ever asked the question "How did our streets get their names?" and actually documented the stories.

Therefore, much of what you will see is conjecture on my part based upon a number of things. In order to ascertain the derivation of any street's name, I've had to consult the history books, subdivision maps, land ownership records, family trees freely available online, and a host of other sources to give a pretty good meaning for the street name.

Some street names are obvious - Park, Mt. View, Main, etc. Some are parts of a series, especially the older ones from the days when Riverside was just starting out (see Presidential Streets). Some are named for the owner/subdivider, or members of his or her family (see Beatty and Merrill). Others are more whimsical, reflecting an interest the subdivider has, such as naming streets for literary characters, English castles, or any of a number of other things. In short, street names reflect many things, most of which are lost in time because no on thinks to document them.

I've done my best to figure out Riverside's main thoroughfares, and a few smaller ones. Some have absolutely eluded me - Chicago Avenue, for instance. Regardless, I hope you enjoy this look at many of our most traveled streets. Do remember, though, that this is a work in progress. If you know the derivation of other street names I've missed, I'd love to hear from you. Please feel free to write me at riversidestreetnameproject@gmail.com.

I'll make this an on-going project, and perhaps come out with a revised book in the future!

The Names

Abilene Road – see Cowboy Streets.

Adams Street – see Presidential Streets.

Aden Way - Named for Aden Clarke who owned the land and built one of the first houses at 4888 Arlington Avenue on the corner of Arlington and Aden Way.[1]

Alessandro Boulevard – This major thoroughfare is a continuation of Alessandro Boulevard in what is today Moreno Valley. Alessandro was the hero of Helen Hunt Jackson's 1884 novel *Ramona*. After its publication, the names in it, especially Ramona and Alessandro, were used for many places. In fact, Moreno Valley was originally known as the Alessandro Valley. In any case, in 1959, a new road was being constructed from the end of Central Avenue to Moreno Valley. That road simply kept the Alessandro name as an extension of it.

Allis Place - This name first appeared on a subdivision map of the early 1950's when heirs of Frank Miller, of Mission Inn fame, subdivided property around the base of Mount Rubidoux before giving the hill to the city as a park. It was named for Miller's daughter, Allis Miller Hutchings.[2]

Amber Avenue – see **Haskell Street**.

Anna Street – see Riverside Trust Company Streets.

Arlington Avenue – Riverside's earliest place names are easy to figure out. There's Riverside, of course, the town by the side of the river. We also have Jurupa and La Sierra, both honoring the nearby Mexican ranchos of their respective names. However, when one delves into the earliest history of Riverside, one comes

Riverside's Parent Navel Orange Tree at the corner of Magnolia and Arlington Avenues, showing a portion of Arlington Ave. circa 1955.

across the name of Arlington associated with the southern portions of the Riverside area. This begs the question – why Arlington?

In all likelihood, the name comes from a fad prevalent during the years immediately following the Civil War of naming or renaming places for Arlington National Cemetery. The cemetery takes its name from Arlington House which was built by George Washington Parke Custis (a son of Martha Washington by a previous marriage), and later owned by Confederate General Robert E. Lee. The Arlington House plantation was confiscated during the Civil War, and Union General Montgomery Meigs, who commanded a garrison on the plantation, commandeered the entire holdings for use as a military cemetery in 1864. In the aftermath of the Civil War, the worst conflagration ever seen until that time, many people sought permanent memorials as a way of honoring the veterans of that war and the many thousands of men who never returned.

One of the main focuses of attention for remembrances of those who died in the Civil War was Arlington National Cemetery. During the period of roughly 1867 to 1900, the Arlington name was affixed to many places. According to Sara Lundberg of the Arlington (Massachusetts) Historical Society, the citizens of West Cambridge, Massachusetts voted to rename their town to Arlington in 1867 to honor the fallen soldiers. Similarly, parks, streets, and other institutions throughout the country, especially in former Union states or areas with large northern populations, soon bore the Arlington name (it should be noted that the town of Arlington, Texas, was named for the Arlington House, NOT Arlington National Cemetery).

Riverside's earliest settlers were almost exclusively people who shared John W. North's ideas of Republican politics, abolitionist ideals, and Methodist religion. Many early settlers had fought for the Union, and had settled on various Riverside lands – one of whom was Henry Hughes, a Civil War officer for whom Hughes Alley in Arlington is named. As more and more people settled in Riverside's southern areas, a move was afoot to give the area its own name. According to early Riverside chronicler Robert Hornbeck, a meeting was held in 1877 wherein a list of names was entered for consideration – the name of Arlington quickly rose to the top and was adopted.

Given Riverside's early settlers, the fact that it was custom at the time to name places throughout the country for Arlington National Cemetery, and there were still deep feelings about the Civil War only twelve years after its end, I believe it can safely be assumed that the naming of Arlington in Riverside is a direct response to all three of the aforementioned items. It seems to be the logical explanation for that name.

Arroyo Drive – This road runs east from Victoria Avenue along the Tequesquite Arroyo for which it is named. The arroyo is Riverside's sunken geographic feature (see also **Victoria Ranch Streets**).

Bandini Avenue – The grantee of the Jurupa Rancho was a mission administrator named Juan Bandini. Although he had little to do with the Jurupa Rancho once he was granted it, his name is strongly affiliated with it.

Banks Drive - This short street within Fairmount Park was named for Walter Banks, a local druggist who served 22 years on the city park board.[3]

Beatty Drive – On November 13, 1923, a subdivision map entitled "Sunnyside Place" was recorded with the City of Riverside showing 98 lots in an area bounded by Central Avenue, Palm

Avenue, Beatty Drive, and Arch Way. The owners of record were William and Elizabeth Beatty of the W. D. Beatty Company of Los Angeles, a realty company. As is usually the case, they named the northern street of this subdivision for themselves.

Beechwood Place – see Wood Streets.

Belinda Drive – Named for Betty and Linda Monroe, daughters of the tract's developer.[4]

Benedict Avenue - In 1919, Charles W. Benedict returned to Riverside and began construction of his castle. This street once ran from today's Alessandro Blvd. to the bridge-gate of the castle which now houses the Teen Challenge organization.[5]

Boundary Lane – In the days prior to the City of Riverside's annexation of the La Sierra area, Boundary Lane used to denote the boundary between the city and county of Riverside.

Bradley Street – Burton P. Bradley owned several acres of orange groves above Arlington Heights and east of the Washington Street southern extension. Earliest record of the street name is from 1911.

Briscoe Street – Named for realtor Rufus J. Briscoe, Jr. who lived on Jurupa Avenue just west of Magnolia and sold many of the lots within the Wood Streets (various articles).

Brockton Avenue – Named for the city of Brockton, Massachusetts. The story starts with Elmer Wallace Holmes. Holmes was born and raised in Brockton and went to work at the age of 10 as a printer's apprentice after his father had died, leaving the family with no means of support. Holmes became a journeyman printer by age 18, but soon after enlisted in the Massachusetts infantry during the Civil War. He fought in the battles of South Mountain, Antietam, and others, and was eventually mustered out at war's end in New Orleans.

After the war, he returned to Massachusetts, entering the newspaper business there. In 1874, he came to Los Angeles because of that scourge of so many people – tuberculosis. Unable to find complete recuperation in the LA region, he was told to move inland, so in the next year he came to Riverside and purchased 27 acres at the northwest corner of Jurupa Avenue and what would become Brockton Avenue.

Elmer Wallace Holmes

Holmes proceeded to plant much of his acreage to oranges, and lined the streets near his home with elm trees, the symbol of his native state. To this area, he gave the name Elm Corners, which seems to have been in use for quite some time. He continued in the newspaper business here, owning or partially owning the Riverside Daily Press for many years, and the San Bernardino Index for about a year.

The old veteran kept in touch with many of his Brockton neighbors and friends, and sent glowing accounts of Riverside, the climate, and the possibilities for riches in citrus raising to his hometown newspaper. Because of this, many Brocktonites joined him here in Riverside. Early settlers in Riverside from Brockton included Edward F. Kingman, George Fullerton, Charles Packard, Aberdeen Keith, George Skinner, and Captain Samuel B. Hinckley.

By 1878, according to several accounts in the Riverside *Press & Horticulturist*, the area north of Jurupa Avenue, south of Bandini, west of what would become Brockton Avenue and east of the river had gained the moniker "Brockton Square" for the many families who had settled there from the Massachusetts namesake. Apparently, it wasn't until about late 1880 when the actual road was put through and given the Brockton name for "Brockton Square" and the many families from that town who lived there.

Brockton Avenue soon became the main route between what was termed the "Government Tract" area of town and downtown. A streetcar line would be placed along Brockton, and most travel into the downtown area occurred on Brockton, which at the time connected to Walnut Street in the downtown area. Magnolia Avenue only went as far north as Arlington Avenue at this time, and would not be completed into downtown until 1913. Around 1933, Walnut Street was renamed to Brockton Avenue, thus greatly lengthening that street.

Brusca Place – Joe Brusca was a long time resident of Riverside and an Italian immigrant. He subdivided three tracts in Riverside, including Brusca Tract No. 3 in July, 1959. The street is named for him.

Buchanan Street – see Presidential Streets.

California Avenue – Named for the State of California, the adopted state of Samuel Cary Evans, developer of the Riverside Land

and Irrigating Company. The main boulevard through the vast acreage of the RL&I was **Magnolia Avenue** (see that). Paralleling Magnolia Avenue was California to the north, and Indiana to the south, the home state of Evans.

Canyon Crest Drive – In 1890, Albert and Alfred Smiley purchased about 200 acres of land southwest of Redlands and developed it with their homes and a botanical garden. They called their new park Canyon Crest Park, although later it would generally be known as Smiley Heights. Over the next several years, the Smileys became good friends with Frank A. Tetley of Riverside. In 1907, Tetley began to develop what the newspapers and many residents were calling a "Smiley Heights in miniature" on the city's eastside. This new development was to be named Monte Vista, with Monte Vista Drive being the main thoroughfare through the new tract. The "miniature Smiley Heights" was to be planted with all sorts of citrus, and would have a number of large-lot residences. A new road was proposed in 1909 to connect this new development to 8th Street (the highway), and so in all likelihood, the name Canyon Crest Drive was given to the road as an homage to Canyon Crest Park and the Smiley Brothers who started it. Later additions to Canyon Crest Drive sent it north to Blaine Street during World War 2 as part of the Canyon Crest housing development for war workers (the former married student housing at UCR), and still later, south through the 1960s subdivisions that have led that section of the city to be dubbed "Canyon Crest."[6]

Carson Road – see Cowboy Streets

Cary Street – see Evans Street.

Castle Reagh Place – Subdivided in 1922 by the R. T. Shea Company. The company did not want to continue the Wood Street naming, so asked Riverside residents to propose names, offering a $50 prize for the best one. Anna Perrine came up with Castle Reagh, beating out over 3,000 other suggestions to win the $50.[7]

Castleman Street - In 1884, John S. Castleman moved with his family from Ontario Province, Canada, to Riverside and became involved in banking and land development. Later his sons Stanley, Pember, and Casey owned land in the area and the street compliments one or all of them.[8]

Castleman Addition Streets – In 1885, John Castleman subdivided acreage on Riverside's east side. There were three north-south trending streets in the subdivision – **Sedgwick Avenue, Kansas Avenue,** and **Ottawa Avenue**. Castleman was Canadian and came from near Ottawa, hence that name. He also had a business partner in the venture (called Kanavel, Castleman & Co.) who was not named on the map, but was in the newspapers of the time. That man was George W. Kanavel who lived in Sedgwick, Kansas. Kanavel was also a major stockholder in Castleman's First National Bank of Riverside.

Cedar Street – see Tree Streets.

Center Street – Named such because it ran through the center of the proposed town of East Riverside, which we today know as Highgrove. In 1886, the East Riverside Land and Water Company mapped their townsite. It did well enough with Gage Canal water but was quickly overshadowed by the larger Riverside town. The main north-south trending street was Iowa Avenue due to the preponderance of Iowans involved in the proposal – see also **Iowa Avenue**.

15

Central Avenue – Central Avenue runs east-west through the center (hence the name) of the area once known as the "Government Tract" in Riverside. The Government Tract was the area between the Jurupa Rancho portion to the north (downtown) and the Arlington area south of Arlington Avenue.

Chapman Place – Named for Deloraine Payson Chapman by his daughters. The Chapman Ranch was on Cypress (New Magnolia). When it was subdivided in 1922 by his daughters, they named it for him. All building plans had to be approved by Henry Jekel.

Chestnut Street – see Tree Streets.

Cheyenne Road – see Cowboy Streets.

Chicago Avenue – <Unknown> - This has defied many hours of research. There was no group of settlers from Chicago on or near the street, the early subdividers of the area including the oldest portions of the street were not from Chicago, and there was no Chicago colony or settlement along the proposed road. What is known is that Chicago Avenue was named sometime between 1885 and 1887. In lieu of anything definitive, I have two theories which should be taken as such:

1. Oscar Wilbur's 1885 "Wilbur Tract" shows northern extensions of Kansas and Ottawa Avenues, and shows a street where Chicago Avenue is, but does not name it. Wilbur is known to visit Chicago on business – it may be homage to whatever business he was conducting there.

2. A very important and well-documented Southern California Citrus Fair was conducted in Chicago during several months of 1886. This citrus fair put Riverside and

its oranges on the map and made for greatly-increased exports of the fruit and more development in town by outsiders. Chicago Avenue may be an homage to that.

Chisholm Road – see Cowboy Streets.

Cimarron Road – see Cowboy Streets.

Cleveland Avenue – Named for President Grover Cleveland. The massive subdivision of Arlington Heights was done during the presidency of Grover Cleveland, hence the name. Other world leaders honored with streets were Queen Victoria and Lord Dufferin (see those).

Coby Court - Named after Coby Dietrick, as his dad was the developer. He starred in basketball at Poly, and later played in the NBA. Laura Lane was named for his sister.[9]

College Avenue – Named for its close proximity to La Sierra College.[10]

Columbia Avenue – This may have been an unofficial road starting in the early 1890s. If so, then it was probably named in honor of the Columbia Exposition of 1893 that celebrated the 400th anniversary of Columbus' "discovery" of America. The reason for it being unofficial is probably just lack of ownership. On November 8, 1899, a statement appears in the Riverside *Daily Press*: "A petition was received from a number of property owners in the neighborhood asking that Columbia avenue be made a county road. This highway runs from Colton avenue [present-day La Cadena] to the Gage canal . . . . and has been traveled for several years."

Copperfield Avenue – see Victoria Highlands Tract Streets.

Coteau Drive – See **Croyance Drive**.

Country Club Drive – This major street through the Canyon Crest area was named for the Canyon Crest Country Club, which opened in January, 1966.

Cover Street (rhymes with Clover) - Although Tom Cover was a well-known figure in the beginnings of Riverside, this street was named for his brother Perry D. Cover who came to Riverside in 1874, settling on land just south of Jurupa Ave. His more famous brother, Tom Cover, had been affiliated with the California Silk Center Association and then with the Southern California Colony Association which founded Riverside.

Cowboy Streets – A later nickname for streets within the neighborhood generally located at the southwest corner of Victoria and Central Avenues. Most of the names of the streets denote people or placenames associated with the Old West and include: **Abilene Road, Carson Road, Cheyenne Road, Chisholm Road, Cimarron Road, Durango Road, Fargo Road, Hickock Way, Iron Hills Way, Laramie Road, Laredo Road, Nevada Way, Pecos Way, Pinkerton Place. Shenandoah Road, Wyoming Way**.

Cridge Street - Named for Alfred Cridge, a carpenter, and his wife Annie Denton Cridge, by Priestly Hall. Hall had purchased and subdivided several acres of land in the area in the late 1880s, and named the street for Cridge, who had come to Riverside in 1871 and built a home on a government claim.

Croyance Drive (and the corresponding **Coteau Drive**) were named by Frank and May Heer of Wishing Well Nursery, after they bought the acreage. They planned to subdivide it. Croyance means belief and Coteau means valley. Both words are of French derivation.[11]

De Anza Avenue - Named for Juan Bautista de Anza, early Spanish military official who came through what would become Riverside County in 1774 in an attempt to find an overland route between Sonora and Mission San Gabriel. One of his many stops was at the location now called Anza Narrows, where he crossed the Santa Ana River. Once it was discovered in the 1920s that de Anza had come through Riverside, Riversiders responded with a street name, a theater, a statue, a park, and an annual community event called De Anza Days.

Del Ray Court – Named for two business partners who subdivided the tract originally in 1926, Delbert Harris and Milton "Ray" McMahan

Denton Street - Named for Professor William Denton, the state geologist of Massachusetts. Denton had two sisters who lived in Riverside in the earliest days, Mrs. Alfred Cridge and Mrs. Seibold. When Priestley Hall made his subdivision in the area, he named this street for one or all of the Dentons.

Dewey Avenue – The derivation of this name is an interesting take on the times. It was previously known as Reservoir Street before 1898. In that year, the United States was in the midst of the Spanish-American War, and people who were following the exploits of Admiral Dewey against the Spanish were wanting to honor him in some way, going so far as to say that California should not give anything else a Spanish name until the war was over. Therefore, on June 10, 1898, several people petitioned the city to change the name of Reservoir Street to Dewey Avenue in honor of Admiral Dewey. The petition was granted.

Dexter Drive - Named for Captain Charles M. Dexter who headed a volunteer committee of Union Veterans of the Civil War in

19

planting trees on Spring Brook bottom land which the city acquired in 1896 incidental to buying quarry sites on North Hill. This led to the establishment of Fairmount Park.

Dickens Avenue – see Victoria Highlands Tract Streets.

Donald Avenue – In 1922, Francis and Loretta Bohr filed the "Arlington Acres" map which subdivided property they had in Arlington along Magnolia just west of Jackson Street. One street was shown coming off of Magnolia, and that was Donald Avenue, in all likelihood named for the Bohr's youngest son.

Dos Casas Place – The term dos Casas means "two houses" in Spanish. At the end of what is Dos Casas Place was two houses, hence the name.

Dufferin Avenue - By the 1870s, a man with the lengthy name of Frederick Temple Hamilton-Temple-Blackwood had already accomplished much in British society, especially in Syria and the middle east. In 1872, he was appointed Governor General of Canada, in which he spent the next several years propelling that position into one of prominence. During his tenure, Prince Edward Island was admitted to Confederation, the Supreme Court of Canada was established, as was the Royal Military College of Canada. In 1871, through birthright, Blackwood was raised to the position of Earl of Dufferin. For the rest of his life, he was known as Lord Dufferin. Matthew Gage, the developer of Arlington Heights and a Canadian by naturalization, would have known of Blackwood, aka Lord Dufferin, and probably admired him greatly. Since two presidential streets paralleled Victoria (see Cleveland Avenue and Lincoln Avenue (2)), Gage probably saw it fitting that the remaining non-presidential street be named for someone prominent in Canadian politics.

Durango Road – see Cowboy Streets.

Edith Avenue – see Victoria Highlands Tract Streets.

Elenor Street – see Magnolia Center Tract streets.

Eliza Street – see Tibbetts Street.

Elizabeth Street – see Magnolia Center Tract streets.

Elliotta Drive - The name comes from William Elliott, who in 1898 drilled a well on the former White Sulphur Springs resort property which he renamed Elliotta Springs. He built a swimming pool and bottled and sold sulphur water from the well.[12]

Elmwood Court and Drive – see Wood Streets.

Elsinore Road (between Victoria Avenue and Glenhaven Avenue) – Originally referred to as Victoria-Elsinore Road because it was the main road connecting Riverside to the city of Elsinore (now Lake Elsinore). The road started at Victoria Avenue and headed east, then southeast along present-day Glenhaven Avenue, then up into the hills south of Riverside. In the community of Mead Valley, there is still a portion of the original road named Old Elsinore Road (see also **Victoria Ranch Streets**).

Evans Street - Samuel Cary Evans Sr. came to Riverside in 1874, becoming a major business leader. His prominent sons Samuel Cary Jr. and Pliny T. Evans, with William Peters, subdivided this portion of Casa Blanca in 1908 giving several streets their own names.[13]

Everest Avenue - Named for Hiram Bond Everest who came to Riverside in 1881 and purchased 100 acres in the Arlington

Panoramic view of orange groves looking east from Victoria Hill, circa 1920. Victoria Avenue runs along most of the bottom of the photo, and Elsinore Road runs east toward Box Springs Mountain. (Author's collection)

area. Being a wealthy oil man he developed citrus groves and operated his own packinghouse. He also owned and operated the Arlington Hotel in downtown.[14]

Fairview Avenue – A descriptive name of the view available from the small hill upon which Fairview started (see **Victoria Ranch Streets**). Fairview soon was extended along the northern side of the Gage Canal and was a service road for the Chase Nursery, which owned much of the land in the region. This road name was retained during the large-scale subdivisions of the early 1960s. However, the small original Fairview Avenue that circled the hill was later changed to **Rawlings Place** (see that).

Fargo Road – see Cowboy Streets.

Fillmore Street – see Presidential Streets.

Gibson Street – see Riverside Trust Company Streets.

Glenwood Drive – This road pays homage to the original name of the Mission Inn, the Glenwood Hotel. It was created in April, 1941 as part of the Mount Rubidoux Park Unit No. 2 tract which was filed by Frank Miller's daughter, Allis Miller Hutchings, in her role as manager of the Mission Inn. Two other streets were shown on the map, Miller and Mission, which did come to fruition, but were instead named **Allis Street** and **Isabella Street** (see those).[15]

Grant Street – see Presidential Streets.

Harding Street – see McKinley Street (2).

Harley John Road – Named for Harley John, the only resident of the road at the time of its naming.[16]

Harrison Street – Named for President William Henry Harrison – see Presidential Streets.

Haskell Street – In 1956, the Haskell Development Company, together with the Shawnee Development Company, recorded the Amberwood Tract. The main road through the tract was named for Haskell. A few years later, additional Amberwood Tracts were recorded leading to **Amber Avenue** for the tract and **Shawnee Avenue** for the Shawnee Development Company.

Hewitt Street - This short street honors John J. Hewitt whose home and grove stood here. He arrived in 1882, became president of the First National Bank of Riverside, and helped organize the cooperative marketing of citrus, now called Sunkist Growers Inc.[17]

Hickock Way – see Cowboy Streets.

Hole Avenue - Named for Willits J. Hole, a wealthy land developer and speculator. In 1909 or 1910 he purchased more than 20,000 acres in today's La Sierra, Arlington, and Norco areas after the land had gone into foreclosure. While he soon sold off large parts of the property, including land that is now part of the city of Norco, Hole was still left with a sizable ranch of approximately 11,500 acres (18 square miles) which he began farming.

Hole was born in Indiana in 1858. As a young man he became the owner of a chair factory, became a contractor and builder, and studied architecture and began designing his own buildings. In 1893 he moved to California due to the health problems of his wife, Mary.

After coming to California, Hole bought 3500 acres in the La Habra Valley. He later sold a part of the land that went on to become the city of La Habra. For that he is known as the "father of La Habra."

In 1912, the wealthy Hole family owned a palatial home in Los Angeles, a winter home in Palm Springs, and a large yacht anchored in Wilmington, but they decided to build a large home on their La Sierra property as well. The home was made with granite stone quarried from Hole's La Sierra property. The new house sat at a higher elevation than most of surrounding land, giving it a sweeping view of the La Sierra Valley.

The home, designed by Arthur Benton, cost $15,000 to build. It was three stories with a red tile roof. It had a veranda across its entire front which shaded the bottom two floors. The main floor included a large drawing room, dining room and a den. Each room had a granite fireplace. A separate wing had a music room with a custom made organ with 1,000 stops. The second floor had four bedrooms, three sleeping porches, and a nursery for the three children of the Hole's only daughter Agnes and her husband Samuel Rindge. The Rindge family moved into the home when it was completed in summer 1913.

While Hole did spend quite a bit of time at his home here, he had a passion for sailing and fishing on his private yacht. He took trips to South America and up the Amazon River and up to the waters off Northern California and Alaska. He even took former president Herbert Hoover on a fishing trip to Mexico, just the two of them and the 16-member crew.

Hole passed away in 1936 and was buried in Evergreen Cemetery. His wife Mary was laid to rest next to him two years later. In 1956 the mansion and the last 60 acres of Hole's original ranch were sold by heirs to the Divine Word Seminary.

Hoover Street - This is on the former land of Martin Hoover who came to Riverside in 1881 after 15 years of mining in California. He served two years as a City Trustee and was elected in 1893 to the original Board of Supervisors when Riverside County was formed.[18] Hoover Street was originally called Robusta.

Named after the very tall *Washingtonia Robusta* palm that stood in the center of the intersection of Magnolia and Robusta/ Hoover. After 10 acres of orange groves were removed and a street added in 1914, the grove home of Martin Hoover (1 of the 3 original Supervisors for Riverside) was fronting Magnolia Avenue but was relocated onto what is now known as Hoover Street. The palm tree Hoover planted had grown so tall that it was a landmark to the people at that time. Removing it just didn't seem right. The name Robusta was changed to Hoover Street (to honor Martin Hoover) in about 1915 or 16. The tree remained at the center of the intersection until the mid-30's.[19]

Horace Street – see Riverside Trust Company Streets.

Houghton Avenue - In 1887 the Riverside Water Company retained R. E. Houghton, a San Francisco attorney specializing in water law. The following year he and John G. North, superintendent of the company and son of Riverside founder John W. North, subdivided the area.[20]

Howard Avenue - This street, part of Hall's Addition subdivision of 1880's, was named for Riley H. Howard. As a friend of the Hall family he came from the East and settled on the north side of the arroyo.[21]

Howe Avenue - Clifford A. Howe built an elaborate Spanish style house in a ten-acre private park. He became the namesake of the street running through the area. With G. G. Merrill he ran a motion picture exhibiting business, operating the Regent, Orphem, and Loring Theaters.[22]

Hughes Alley - Once known as Hughes Lane this street was named for Henry Luke Hughes, Union Veteran of the Civil War, who once farmed along this alley.[23]

Huntington Drive – This is the road that goes both up and down Mt. Rubidoux. It was named in honor of Henry Huntington, President of the Pacific Electric Railroad. Mr. Huntington was a big investor in Riverside, especially at the behest of Frank Miller. He invested in the Mission Inn's original 1903 wing, and also funded much of the construction of the road that ultimately would be named for him.

Huntington Drive, circa 1910.

Indian Hill Road – For many years, what is generally known today as Little Mt. Rubidoux was called Indian Hill. This in turn was named as such due to the Spring Rancheria, one of at least three Indian villages that existed in what would become Riverside at the time of Riverside's founding. Indian Hill Road actually started as Aurora Drive, its name being changed later.

Indiana Avenue – Named for the State of Indiana, the birth state of Samuel Cary Evans, developer of the Riverside Land and Irrigating Company. The main boulevard through the

27

11235. Aurora Drive, Riverside, Cal.

Aurora Drive as it appeared circa 1910. Its present name is Indian Hill Drive.

vast acreage of the RL&I was **Magnolia Avenue** (see that). Paralleling Magnolia Avenue was California to the north, (Evans' adopted state) and Indiana to the south.

Iowa Avenue - In 1886, the East Riverside Land and Water Company mapped their townsite of East Riverside. Its main north-south street was Iowa Avenue due to the preponderance of Iowans involved in the proposal. As development continued to the south, Iowa Avenue continued to be extended (see also **Center Street**).

Iron Hills Way – see Cowboy Streets.

Irving Street – see Riverside Trust Company Streets.

Isabella Street - Named for Frank Miller's first wife Isabella Hardenberg or his granddaughter Isabella Hutchings.[24]

Jack B. Clarke Drive – On January 14, 1986, Jack B. Clarke Sr. became the first African-American to be elected to the Riverside City Council, handily overcoming his opponent in the second ward race, Bud Stone. When Clarke left, the Council renamed this short street on the city's Eastside for Councilman Clarke.

Jackson Street – see Presidential Streets.

Jane Street – see Riverside Trust Company Streets.

Jarvis Street - Jarvis Bradley, grandson of Dr. Joseph Jarvis, owned ten acres of walnut trees south of Rubidoux Avenue. When the area was subdivided, the south boundary was named Jarvis.[25]

Jefferson Street – see Presidential Streets.

Junelle Avenue – see Magnolia Center Tract streets.

Jurupa Avenue – This road is named for the fact that it is the southern boundary of the Jurupa Rancho in Riverside. The Jurupa Rancho was the main Mexican-era land grant to encompass lands within the future Riverside. In 1838, the Jurupa Rancho was deeded to Juan Bandini (see **Bandini Avenue**). The word Jurupa is a local Indian place name meaning "place of the sagebrush."[26]

Knoefler Drive – Named for local bee-keeping family the Knoeflers.

La Cadena Drive - La Cadena Drive is the most direct surface street linking Riverside to Colton and San Bernardino. For years it was the main thoroughfare between the three cities, and that was by design, not accident.

The earliest references to the road appear in 1878 when it was dubbed the Ranch Line Road because it was located along the eastern line of the Jurupa Rancho. On various subdivision maps of the area, it was simply referred to as "County Road." By 1880, it had assumed the name Colton Avenue since it started in Riverside and led to Colton. Thirty-five years later, it had become the main north-south route linking Riverside to Colton and San Bernardino, and was becoming the object of attention of Clinton Hickok, one of many people trying to beautify Riverside.

Hickok owned a house at the corner of Strong Street and Colton Avenue. He had advocated for the improvement of Colton Avenue since 1913 when he got the city of Riverside and his Colton Avenue Improvement Association to plant over 200 trees along the west side of Colton Avenue. Because Colton Avenue was the entryway into Riverside by the Pacific Electric Railway, it was vitally important to Hickok and others that the road look its best so it could become one of Riverside's showcase entry points. In addition to the many trees, a park was added at the county line, and shrubs were eventually planted along the avenue also.

Soon, these improvement efforts, combined with others to straighten the road, caught the attention of similar civic-minded people in Colton and San Bernardino. Hickok had become president of the Riverside Chamber of Commerce, and so he advocated a larger role for Colton Avenue with the three cities. By the spring of 1915, there was a growing movement to rename the road through all of the cities. On March 31, a dinner meeting was held at the Mission Inn and attended by representatives of all three cities. The object of the meeting was to find an appropriate name for the new showcase road. "Mission Road" and "Avenue del Rio" were ideas that came up, but no consensus was made. Nearly two weeks later, on April 12, another meeting was held in the Anderson Hotel in Colton. At this time, delegates from the Riverside and San Bernardino Chambers of Commerce, together with the Colton Merchants' Association, decided on La Cadena Drive. La cadena means "chain" in Spanish, and it was felt that La Cadena Drive would be the chain that linked the three cities together. This was immediately adopted by the group, which began advocating for the name change.

Over the ensuing months, the cities of Riverside, Colton, and San Bernardino, together with the counties of Riverside and San Bernardino, all changed the name of the road to La Cadena Drive. It was improved with concrete and more landscaping and became a true showplace avenue in the area. Most of these improvements were removed when the 91 freeway was constructed in the late 1950s, but for many years, La Cadena Drive was the pride of Riverside and was its gateway to points north.

La Sierra Avenue – The La Sierra (Sepulveda) and La Sierra (Yorba) Ranchos were decreed in the last days of Mexican rule in California. Ever since then, the area generally southwest of Riverside has been known as the La Sierra area of the city. The origins of La Sierra Avenue lie in the Presidential Streets (see that). Originally, La Sierra Avenue was Taylor Street in the presidential progression, named for Zachary Taylor. In October, 1918, a petition was given to the County of Riverside (La Sierra was in the county at the time) asking that the name of Taylor be changed to Holden Avenue for that section north of Magnolia. The petition was granted.[27] In October, 1957, several land owners in the area petitioned to change the name of Holden/Taylor to La Sierra Avenue, paying homage to the La Sierra Ranchos. This led to some controversy because that would remove one main road from the presidential progression. That controversy, however, was overshadowed by the impending construction of today's SR 91 freeway. Offramps were being planned at Tyler Street and Taylor Street. Needless to say, that would have led to much confusion. By March, 1958, the name had been changed to La Sierra Avenue.

Laramie Road – see Cowboy Streets.

Larchwood Place – see Wood Streets.

Laredo Road – see Cowboy Streets.

Laura Lane – Named after Laura Dietrick, as her dad was the developer. **Coby Court** is named for her brother.[28]

Lemon Street – see Tree Streets.

Lila Street – Named for Lila Jones as part of the Jones Tract. The Jones Tract was filed in 1950 by Lila and her husband Kermit (see also **Susan Street**).

Lime Street – see Tree Streets.

Lincoln Avenue – Named for President Abraham Lincoln as part of the overall map subdividing the Arlington Heights area. The three streets laid out as part of this tract that paralleled Lincoln were Victoria, Cleveland, and Dufferin, all named for contemporary national leaders. It may be simply that the last one, Lincoln Avenue, was named in deference to the slain president because Lincoln Street (see that) was such a short street and very far away from both Riverside and Arlington.

Lincoln Street – see Presidential Streets.

Linden Street – Probably another tree street (see that section). Linden is known botanically as *Tilia Americana*.

Linwood Place – see Wood Streets.

Locust Street – see Tree Streets.

Loring Drive - This street was part of the 1906 subdivision of Huntington Park in which Charles M. Loring, Henry E. Huntington, and Frank Miller were stockholders. Loring, who lived primarily in Minneapolis, was an enthusiastic winter resident of Riverside.[29]

Luther Street – See Tibbetts Street.

Madison Street – see Presidential Streets.

Magnolia Avenue – Originally to be called Bloomingdale, Magnolia Avenue was named because the original plans for this boulevard called for Magnolia trees to be planted along its length. When the cost of Magnolia trees was found to be prohibitive, palm and pepper trees were planted along much of the avenue, and Magnolias were placed only at the main intersections. Magnolia Avenue was the main boulevard through the lands of the Riverside Land and Irrigating Company, established by Samuel Cary Evans in 1874. The boulevard was meant to be a grand advertising mechanism for showing off the lands for sale.

Magnolia Center Tract Streets – In 1929, three women, Elenor Vanderslice, her sister-in-law Nora Vanderslice, and Nora's sister Zoe Jagers, subdivided land at the southeast corner of Jurupa and Magnolia into both residential and commercial lots. Three streets were created – **Elenor Street** for Elenor Vanderslice, and **Elizabeth Street** and **Junelle Street** for the two young daughters of Zoe Jagers.

Main Street – This should be obvious, but Main Street is the main street in town, usually the business center of a town. It was in Riverside's case when it started and generally lasted through the post-war era.

Marguerita Street – see Riverside Trust Company Streets.

Market Street – While it is difficult to determine with certainty

33

the origins of Riverside's Market Street, all circumstantial evidence seems to point to it being named for Market Street in San Francisco. First, it is the only north-south trending street downtown (besides Main) not named for a tree. Second, on the original "Town of Riverside" map, it is one of four streets (Main, Seventh, and Eighth being the others) shown as a wider thoroughfare. Third, Market Street in San Francisco is a major artery in that city, being the distinctive dividing line between the northern section laid out on compass directions, and the southern section laid out on Mission Avenue and at a distinct angle to the northern section. Fourth, John North's main financier was Charles Felton, who was from San Francisco and who maintained an office there. Finally, the party that accompanied North to found what became Riverside went first to San Francisco and established themselves there while trips were made to examine sites for the colony. In other words, there was quite a tie between San Francisco and Riverside at the earliest timeframe and Market Street probably was an homage to the older city.

Riverside's

Main Street
Magnolia Avenue
&
Market Street

as seen in

Vintage
Postcards

Main st., Looking North, Riverside.

Main Street, Riverside, Cal.

75 Main St., Riverside, Cal.

(Left, above) Main Street looking north from 9th, circa 1900.
(Left, center) Main Street looking south from between 6th and 7th, circa 1905.
(Left, below) Main Street looking north from 9th, circa 1910.
(Above, top) Main Street looking north from 9th, 1943.
(Above) Main Street looking north from 10th, circa 1956.

Magnolia Ave., Riverside, Cal.

(Above) Magnolia Avenue, circa 1905.
(Right, above) An auto excursion on Magnolia Avenue, circa 1910.
(Right, center) A trolley prepares to turn right from Magnolia Avenue onto
Arlington Avenue to head downtown via Brockton Avenue, circa 1902.
(Right, below) "Magnolia Center" - The intersection of Brockton, Central, and
Magnolia Avenues looking northwest, circa 1930. (All postcards author's collection)

Magnolia Avenue,
Riverside, California.
"On the Salt Lake Route."

Magnolia Ave.,
Riverside, Cal.

Geographical Center City of Riverside
Magnolia Center

39

Market Street looking south from 8th, circa 1955.

Market Street looking north from 9th, 1970s.

41

Marley Drive – see Victoria Highlands Tract Streets.

Mary Street – see Riverside Trust Company Streets.

Maplewood Place – see Wood Streets.

Maude Street – see Riverside Trust Company Streets.

McCray Street – According to the newspapers of the time, the very first new improvements to go in along "New Magnolia" was a small tract called the "Palm Addition." "Palm Addition" was recorded in December, 1908, and included several small lots between Palm Avenue and Brockton, divided by a newly-installed McCray Street. Lots of fanfare accompanied the new improvements, including concrete curb and gutter plus sidewalks for the anticipated residences. The concrete contractor that was awarded the job was the McCray Cement Company of Los Angeles, the apparent namesake of McCray Street. Considering that the Rubidoux Building Company did the subdivision, McCray was probably a friend or associate.

McKenzie Street – Named before 1909 for Roderick McKenzie, who, with Robert Pedley, sold real estate in the Arlington area in the 1900s and 1910s.

McKinley Street (1) – On September 6, 1901, President William McKinley was assassinated, and the whole nation went into mourning. Several cities began to name or rename parks and streets for the martyred president. At the same time, the Riverside Land and Irrigating Company was looking to move Johnson Street in its **Presidential Streets** progression a bit west so that the street would lead up the center of a small arroyo. Instead, they opted to vacate and remove Johnson Street (President Johnson had been quite unpopular and was nearly impeached). In November, 1901, the land company submitted the "Map of the Riverside Land Company's Foothill Tract" showing two new streets, one leading up the arroyo to be named McKinley Street and another along the Santa Fe Railroad named **Sampson Avenue** (see that). This map was approved, Johnson Street was forgotten, and McKinley Street joined the lattice work of presidential streets despite the fact that the new street's name was quite out of order (See also **Presidential Streets**).

McKinley Street (2) – This McKinley Street is a small residential street going between Arlington Avenue and Diana Street just east of Washington Street. It was developed in 1925 as part of the Orange Acres subdivision. At the same time, **Harding Street** was developed also. Although it is speculation, both President McKinley and President Warren G. Harding were the last two presidents to die in office at the time of the subdivision. This fact, together with their location at the beginning of the Presidential Streets may account for the names.

Metcalf Lane – This street used to be Ridge Road but was changed to Metcalf in honor of the Metcalf family that used to own the orange orchards from Golden to Hallmark.[30]

Merrill Avenue – On September 8, 1925, a subdivision map called "Venetian Square" was recorded showing 98 lots. This tract was bounded by Beatty Drive, Palm Avenue, Arch Way, and Dewey Avenue. Through the middle of this tract ran Merrill Avenue. Initial speculation about Merrill Avenue had to do with Samuel Merrill who was the subdivider of what is today Highgrove, plus much of the Bloomington-Fontana area. However, that was not true. The owners of record for the Venetian Square map were William E. and Matilda Merrill,

William being listed alternately as a building contractor and a real estate agent in Riverside.

Mission Inn Avenue - Named in 1993 for Riverside's Nationally-Registered Historic Hotel, the Mission Inn, which faces the avenue. Previous name = 7th Street.

*A Fred W. Martin hand-tinted postcard of the
Mission Inn in downtown Riverside.*

Monroe Street – see Presidential Streets.

Mulberry Street – see Tree Streets.

Nelson Street – In 1926, a map named "Nelson Square" was filed along New Magnolia. This small tract had 27 lots and was located between Magnolia and Brockton Avenues. The new connecting road on the tract was named Nelson Street, the entire subdivision being completed by August and Hulda Nelson for whom the street is named. August, a native of Sweden, owned a shoe repair business on 8th Street in downtown Riverside, and the couple lived close to the subdivision that bears their name.

Nevada Way – see Cowboy Streets.

Nixon Drive – The former Canal Drive was renamed in February, 1954 to honor then-Vice Present Richard Nixon.[31]

Norton Place - Charles T. Norton and his brother Richard operated a ten-acre nursery facing Brockton Avenue near Rice Road. Their name is memorialized by this short street.[32]

Numbered Streets – Downtown's east-west tending streets are all numbered from 1 to 14. This is one of several sets of "series" streets that are often the result of having to name several streets all at once. Other examples in Riverside include the **Tree Streets** and the **Presidential Streets** (see those).

Nye Avenue – In 1926, Charles and Maude Nye subdivided a small tract called Arlington Gardens on Polk Street between Magnolia and Indiana. They added one street just east of Polk, and named it for themselves.

Oakwood Place – see Wood Streets.

Olivewood Avenue - On Monday, February 18, 1889, the Riverside Board of Trustees approved the engineering work for "a new avenue 66 feet wide [to be] laid out from Prospect avenue to intersect Arlington avenue . . . . and that it be known as "Olivewood" avenue." That road was constructed very soon after, and went as far as Olivewood Cemetery, its namesake. Olivewood Avenue is in all likelihood the origin of the Wood Streets (see that), in that it is a tree name with the suffix "wood" attached, like all the other Wood Streets roads are.

45

Riverside's Numbered Streets

Seventh st., looking West, Riverside, Cal

SEVENTH STREET FROM MAIN.   RIVERSIDE, CALIFORNIA.

in Vintage Postcards

8th. st., looking West, Riverside, Cal.

SEVENTH ST., RIVERSIDE, CALIFORNIA

(Left, above) Seventh Street looking west from the Mission Inn, circa 1905.
(Left, center) Seventh Street looking west from the top of the
Rubidoux Building, circa 1920s.
(Left, below) Seventh Street looking west from Orange, circa 1955.
(Above, top) Eighth Street looking west from Orange, circa 1905.
(Above, below) Eighth Street (erroneously labeled Seventh Street)
looking west at Main Street, 1930s.

Orange Street – see Tree Streets.

Orange Vista Way – Named for the Orange Vista Tract that subdivided residential lots at the northwest corner of Sierra and Palm. Orange Vista Way had a terminus at Harris Street, named for one of the principals behind the subdivision. Harris has since been renamed to Fig Street.

Osburn Place – Named for Robert Osburn, citrus rancher, realtor, and polo enthusiast of the late 1800s-early 1900s. His daughter, Virginia, was a realtor who subdivided her father's grove on the east end of the Wood Streets. She renamed the earlier, existing Fir Street to Osburn Place in honor of her father.[33]

Pachappa Drive/Pachappa Hill (Road) – Both roads are named for their proximity to Pachappa Hill, a geographic landmark in central Riverside. Originally, though, Pachappa Hill was not the one named such today – it was actually what we today call Mt. Rubidoux. The local Indians called Mt. Rubidoux Pachappa (pronounced PAH-cha-pa), meaning "the place where the water bends."[34] This is in keeping with the distinctive bend the Santa Ana River makes a short distance to the north. Why the switch in names from Mt. Rubidoux to present-day Pachappa Hill? It had to do with floating the boundary of the Rancho Jurupa to incorporate more land into it. The legal description of the Rancho Jurupa indicated that one corner of the rancho was a "high, detached hill," and from there, the line would go "11 leagues west along the river." People familiar with Riverside know that there is no river near present-day Pachappa Hill, but there is next to Mt. Rubidoux. In essence, the surveyors found another "high, detached hill" to take their measurements from, and incorporated most of what is today downtown Riverside into the Rancho Jurupa.

Palmyrita Avenue – In 1889, Woodruff McKnight, son of Rep. Robert Knight of Pennsylvania, purchased land on the city's east side and began building a large residence. The McKnights dubbed their estate "Rancho Palmyrita," hence the name of the street.[35] Palmyrita seems to be a Hispanic version of Palmyra, the ancient city of the Levant now part of Syria. There is also a Palmyra in Pennsylvania, but it is nowhere near Pittsburg where the McKnights were from. Why the McKnights chose Palmyra is not known.

Panorama Road – Undoubtedly named because of the wide views of downtown Riverside and the Eastside neighborhood. It was formerly Chase Road, but in 1953, the Planning Commission changed it to Panorama at the behest of Anne Evans Brown, daughter of Pliny Evans. Her son, Michael Brown, indicated that the family had lost a lot of property with the coming of the freeway too.[36]

Pecos Way – see Cowboy Streets.

Peggy Lane – Named for Peggy Savage, wife of the contractor who built the homes along it.[37]

Peters Street - William L. Peters, mayor of Riverside from 1912-14, was one of the subdividers of this area. See Evans Street.[38]

Philbin Avenue - Philip Philbin was the signatory on the second highest bid for Camp Anza, on the western edge of Riverside. **Philip Avenue**, off of Rutland Avenue south of Arlington Avenue, was for Philbin's first name.[39]

Philip Avenue – See **Philbin Avenue**.

Pierce Street – see Presidential Streets.

Pine Street – see Tree Streets.

Pinkerton Place – see Cowboy Streets.

Pliny Street – see Evans Street.

Polk Street – see Presidential Streets.

Presidential Streets – In large-scale developments of the time, it was typical to name streets in a series, such as numbers, owners of the land company, trees, etc. One of the most popular series was the United States presidents. The Riverside Land and Irrigating Company was no exception, and when they laid out the main boulevard through their lands (see **Magnolia Avenue**), they crossed their main boulevard with streets named for the presidents. Curiously, though, there are errors in the presidential order, and some have changed. The series starts, naturally, with Washington. The next president was John Adams, and this one was skipped in the street naming. The next two presidents were Thomas Jefferson and James Madison, but they are reversed in the street order. Likewise, the next two presidents after Madison were James Monroe and John Quincy Adams, and their streets are similarly reversed (with Riverside's Adams Street representing John Quincy Adams, not his father John Adams). Why these two sets of streets are reversed is not known, but such an error seems strange given the reverence for the presidents at the time. Starting with **Jackson Street**, named for president Andrew Jackson, all the rest of the streets are in presidential order down to **Grant Street**, which was the last of the presidential streets since U. S. Grant was president when the map of the Riverside Land and Irrigating Company was produced in 1874. In subsequent years, two of the presidential streets were renamed – **La Sierra Avenue** for Taylor Street and **McKinley Street** for Johnson Street (see those).

Adams st., Riverside, Cal.

Primrose Drive – The original name for this small street in Arlington was Hoag Avenue. This was created by the Map of the Primrose Subdivision in October, 1907. Why that name was chosen is not known, but in 1948, fully 40 years after the subdivision and street, residents petitioned the city to change the street's name to Primrose Drive (probably after the subdivision), stating that, "the new name was more attractive than the old and would benefit them and the street."[40]

Prince Albert Drive – In late 1927, Robert Lee Bettner subdivided land on the north ridge of the Tequesquite Arroyo under the name of "Queen's Terrace." However, Queen Victoria already had a boulevard named for her, so instead Bettner chose to name the main street through his subdivision Prince Albert, for Victoria's husband.

Ramona Drive – Throughout Southern California, many places are named for Ramona, the fictional heroine of a book by the same name. *Ramona* was written in 1884 by Helen Hunt Jackson to be a romantic testimonial to the treatment of the California Indians, not unlike what Harriet Beecher Stowe had tried to do for enslaved African-Americans with her novel *Uncle Tom's Cabin*. Instead, because Mrs. Jackson died just 9 months after the book's publication, it became the de facto history of Southern California and led to the whole romanticized view of California's Spanish past, with the colorful missions, helpful padres, and docile Indians. With the huge popularity of *Ramona*, many places were given that name, including the northernmost Wood Street.

Randall Road - From the 1880's to the early 1900's, Leland Randall lived on Pine Street between First and Houghton. He owned a pear orchard in the area now partly occupied by the Fairmount

This idyllic citrus crate label idolizes the fictional Ramona. Ramona brought about the romanticized Spanish past of California and led to many place names throughout the region.

Park rose garden. Randall Road would have been a route from his home to his orchard.[41]

Rawlings Place – Named for Gary Rawlings, one-time owner of the older home near the top of the small hill right were Central Avenue begins to turn southeast (see also **Fairview Avenue**).

Redwood Drive – see Tree Streets.

Rice Road - In 1880, Charles T. Rice acquired property on the south rim of Tequesquite Arroyo at Brockton Avenue. He grew citrus fruits planted partly on terraces and is believed to have introduced this practice to the Riverside area, thus accounting for the name Terracina Drive.[42]

Riverside Trust Company Streets - Matthew Gage was the president of the Riverside Trust Company, subdivider of the Arlington Heights area in 1890. As such, Gage named many of the streets on the far east end of Arlington Heights for relatives. **Jane Street** and **Gibson Street** were named for his wife, Jane Gibson Gage. Others, such as **Anna Street, Horace Street, Maude Street,** and **Marguerita Street**, were named for his children. Also included in this were **Irving Street** (for William Irving, married to Gage's sister Eliza), and **Mary Street** (named for his brother Robert's wife).[43] See also **Victoria Avenue, Dufferin Avenue, and Cleveland Avenue.**

Roosevelt Street – In all likelihood named for President Theodore Roosevelt who was president when the "Artesia Addition to Arlington" map was filed in March, 1903, by George Frost, P. T. Evans, and Kingsbury Sanborn. This map created the street along with 26 lots along it.

Rosewood Place – see Wood Streets.

Rubidoux Avenue – Louis Rubidoux (properly spelled Robidoux) bought a large portion of the Jurupa Rancho from Juan Bandini in 1839. When the Rubidoux portion of it was surveyed, the southern lines did not match up exactly, and a line tending to the northwest became the southern boundary of Rubidoux's portion. This small line, extending to the Santa Ana River, became the future Rubidoux Avenue in Riverside's Grand Neighborhood

Rudicill Street - This street name honors Henry J. Rudisill (note difference in spelling) first secretary of the Riverside Land & Irrigating Company and brother-in-law of S. C. Evans Sr. Rudisill promoted the citrus industry and in 1886 helped bring the Santa Fe Railroad into Riverside.[44]

Rumsey Drive - In 1900, Cornelius Earle Rumsey retired from management of the National Biscuit Company and moved to Riverside as a health seeker. He invested extensively in citrus land, planting much of it above Victoria Avenue. This street runs through one portion of his former property.[45]

Russell Street - William P. Russell came to Riverside in 1871 and became a pioneer in citrus cultivation. He served as a city trustee in 1883. His home and nursery were located along Russell Street.[46]

Sampson Avenue – This road, created by the "Map of the Riverside Land Company's Foothill Tract" appears to be named for another major figure in the news of late 1901, Admiral William Sampson (the other being President McKinley). Admiral Sampson was a distinguished naval officer generally known for his victory in the Battle of Santiago de Cuba during the Spanish–American War. Admiral Sampson had set the framework for the destruction of the Spanish fleet, but it was actually carried out by another Admiral, William Scot Schley. Sampson did not acknowledge Schley's role in the conflict, and Schley appealed to the Board of Inquiry. This battle of egos was being waged during late 1901, with many people taking up sides for either Sampson or Schley. It was into this fray that the Riverside Land Company jumped when it seems to have named the new east-west street for Admiral Sampson.

San Simeon Way – This street started as early as the 1880s as School Street. By the early 1950s, with the development of the Sun Gold Terrace tracts and the Brockton Arcade, the name apparently no longer suited the area. The developers of Sun Gold Terrace Tracts 1 and 2 named their new streets after national and state parks, such as Yellowstone, Tahoe, and Yosemite. However, the eastern entrance to their new tract still bore the name School Street. On July 22, 1952, the Riverside City Council, probably at the request of the developers, renamed School Street between Brockton Avenue and De Anza Avenue to San Simeon Way in keeping with the national and state park theme.

Shawnee Avenue – see **Haskell Street**.

Shenandoah Road – see Cowboy Streets.

Stanley Court – Named for longtime UCR professor John Stanley.[47]

Stotts Street - Guy P. Stotts was a blacksmith and orange grower in the Arlington area. He owned land on Magnolia Avenue near Jackson and in 1910 and created the "Stott's Tract," naming the street after his family.

Streeter Avenue - Named for Henry Streeter, an early resident of Riverside whose property was at the northeast corner of Streeter and Central Avenues. Streeter later became the State Senator from the area, and is best remembered as introducing the bill to create Riverside County into the State Senate in 1893.

Strong Street - Dwight S. Strong, a musician in the Civil War, came to Riverside in 1873 and settled in the Highgrove area. Later he purchased acreage where Strong Street is located.[48]

Sunnyside Drive – Assumedly, "Sunnyside" is a play on Riverside. The origins of the name are not readily available, but what is known is that the term Sunnyside was given to the area originally known as the Government Tract from the earliest days.

Susan Street – Named for Susan (Jones) Garat as part of the Jones Tract. The Jones Tract was done in 1950 by her parents, Kermit and Lila Jones (see also **Lila Street**).

Terracina Drive – see Rice Road.

Tibbetts Street – In April and May of 1887, Luther and Eliza Tibbetts subdivided land at the northeast corner of Magnolia Avenue and Arlington Avenue. In this "Tibbetts Tract," they created Tibbetts Street named for them. This map also created Eliza Street on the east, which was soon made into the extension of Brockton Avenue between downtown and Arlington Avenue. Luther Street, a few blocks north, survives and was named for Mr. Tibbetts.

Trautwein Avenue - Alfred Philip Trautwein, a highly-skilled and educated engineer specializing in ice-making equipment, and his wife Mary Emma Hendrick Trautwein, appear to be the people behind this name. Mary was the daughter of Eli Hendrick of the large Hendrick Ranch in Moreno Valley. Alfred was hired by Eli Hendrick to help design things for Hendrick's manufacturing plant in Pennsylvania, and then later to build an ice plant in California to help with the orange shipping industry.

In 1909, Eli Hendrick died and control of the estate went to his two daughters, Mary and her sister Lillian, and their combined eight children, but not their spouses. It was estimated that the ranch consisted of just under 17,600 acres, or 27½ square miles, at that time.

Alfred Trautwein died in 1914. Mary, being the older sister of the family, assumed leadership of the family as it pertained to the land holdings. Throughout the years, much of the acreage was devoted to ranching, but apparently it was not very profitable.

In 1941, the U.S. Government condemned about 950 acres of land to be used for an enlargement of March Field. Subsequent sales greatly reduced the lands.

Interestingly, the Trautweins seem to have been absentee landowners. Mary spent most of her life in Pennsylvania, traveling out here to visit the property on at least one occasion when she and her daughter Caroline drove cross-country in the late 1920s.

Mary Emma Hendrick Trautwein died in 1966 at age 105. By that time, the family's holdings were estimated at just over 6,600 acres. Those lands have subsequently been sold also.

For absentee landowners, the Trautwein family left a marked imprint on the development of the Riverside-Moreno Valley area.[49]

Tree Streets. In the early days of Southern California, when Riverside was in its infancy, it was common practice in new towns to name streets for various trees, bushes, etc. Why? Because owners of these new towns were marketing land to people who lived not here in Southern California, but in the Mid-west, East Coast, New England, etc. In those locations, many people considered the West to be one large expanse of waterless desert where nothing could grow. To mitigate that, many streets were named for various trees that could grow, given irrigation water. Riverside was no different – and Riverside's downtown is crossed by many streets bearing the name of a tree (Redwood, Pine, Cedar, Locust, Walnut, Chestnut, Orange, Lemon, Lime, Mulberry, Vine).

Tyler Street – see Presidential Streets.

University Avenue – Renamed from 8th Street around 1969 because it leads to UCR on Riverside's far east end.

Van Buren Boulevard – see Presidential Streets.

The center of campus at UCR - namesake for Riverside's University Avenue.

Victoria Avenue – This is the showcase boulevard for the Arlington Heights area, and was patterned after Magnolia Avenue which parallels it to the north. Due to the large amount of British investment that Matthew Gage procured to develop the Arlington Heights area, he opted to name the main boulevard for Queen Victoria, the very popular reigning monarch of the time (see also **Riverside Trust Company Streets**).

Victoria Highlands Tract Streets – When Don and Berenice Wilson subdivided land just south of the southeast corner of Arlington Avenue and Victoria Avenue in 1959, Don Wilson gave his wife the opportunity to name the streets. She selected **Edith Avenue** after her mother. Both Berenice and Edith loved reading Charles Dickens, so Berenice selected Dickens characters to fill out the list – **Copperfield Avenue, Dickens Avenue,** and **Marley Drive.**[50]

Victoria Ave., Riverside, Cal.

Looking south on Victoria Avenue, circa 1905. Myrtle Street would be off to the right, and Elsinore Road to the left.

Victoria Ranch Streets – In October, 1901, the Chase Nursery subdivided nearly 200 acres of land near the northeast corner of Central and Victoria Avenues. In this map, they introduced **Arroyo Drive** (because it runs along the southern edge of the arroyo), **Elsinore Road** (because it led to the town of Elsinore – see Elsinore Road), and **Fairview Avenue** around a small hill on the southeast corner of the tract.

Vine Street – see Tree Streets.

Walnut Street (now Brockton Avenue downtown) – see Tree Streets.

Pepper and Palm Trees, Walnut Street, Riverside, Cal.

Washington Street – see Presidential Streets.

Watkins Drive – Dr. Gordon S. Watkins was the first provost of the newly-established University of California at Riverside, and served in that capacity from 1949 to 1956. Watkins Hall on campus is similarly named for him.

Wells Avenue - In all likelihood, Wells Avenue was named for prominent La Sierra resident Jesse Warren Wells.

Jesse Wells was born on September 1, 1883, in the Territory of South Dakota. When he was about eight years old, his family moved from the Dakota Territory to California and settled in Rincon, the town that was ultimately the site of today's Prado dam and reservoir.

After graduating from high school at age 18, Jesse moved to the La Sierra area of Riverside and was hired by the Citizens National Bank in Riverside. In 1913, he was promoted to the position of cashier and was sent to the Arlington Branch where he remained until 1949, retiring as manager of that branch. In addition, he spent more than 25 years on the board of the Citizens National Bank.

Wells was very active in community affairs. He was a longtime member of the Arlington Lions Club, the Chamber of Commerce, and other civic groups. In the mid-1920s, several of his cohorts encouraged him to run for city council from the La Sierra area. Not only did Wells win the election in 1926, he went on to serve 12 years on the city council for the sixth ward, being defeated for reelection in 1938.

In addition to serving the people and area of La Sierra, Wells was also quite active in civic affairs in Rialto. He was on the board of the Rialto Chamber of Commerce for several years along with their Lion's Club.

The first mention of Wells Avenue is in 1925, right before Jesse Wells became a city councilman but well after he had established himself as a banker and civic leader. It appears that Wells Avenue was developed as part of the La Sierra Gardens subdivision in the Wells/Hole area in 1924. Subsequent subdivisions have extended the street to the east.

Whittier Place - In return for improving White Park in the 1880's, Dr. Clark Whittier received half of the original four block site.

He had agreed to build a sanitarium, but he died unexpectedly and his wife sold the property as residential lots, Whittier Place being one of the resulting streets.[51]

Wohlstetter Street - Charles Wohlstetter was one of the financiers who helped Philip Philbin with the purchase of the Camp Anza property in 1946.[52]

Wong Way (Street) - This short street, originally called Wong Way, was named somewhat facetiously but it honors George Wong who owned and lived in Riverside's early Chinatown until his death in 1974.[53] Around 2010, it was renamed to Wong Street.

Wood Streets – The Wood Streets is a neighborhood in Riverside, characterized by the fact that most (but not all) of the streets in the area end in –wood (e.g. Maplewood, Rosewood, Oakwood, Linwood, Elmwood, Beechwood, and Larchwood). These names are additions to the "Tree Streets" of downtown in that they also advertise, in a way, the broad range of trees that can be grown in the area. Origin of the Wood Streets has in the past been given to a Dr. Edward Wood who subdivided Homewood Court, this this seems to be a correlation-equals-causation error as Dr. Wood does not show up on any other subdivisions. True origin of the Wood Streets is probably **Olivewood Avenue** (see that).

Woodie Way – On October 22, 2019, the Riverside City Council voted to change the name of Prospect Avenue between 15th Street and Saunders Way to honor Waudieur "Woodie" Rucker-Hughes, a longtime activist and educator who led the Riverside branch of the NAACP for two decades.[54]

Wyoming Road – see Cowboy Streets.

Endnotes

1   Bryan Roby, Facebook post, May 4, 2024.

2   Joan Hall, Riverside Bicentennial Place Name Map, 1976.

3   *Ibid.*

4   Bryan Roby, Facebook post, May 4, 2024.

5   Joan Hall, Riverside Bicentennial Place Name Map, 1976.

6   "Celebrate the Smileys!" (https://www.akspl.org/news-events/patron-saints-day/, accessed July 9, 2024); Riverside *Enterprise*, June 2, 1907 et al; Katherine Evans (great-grandniece of Frank A. Tetley), various personal communications with the author, June, 2024.

7   Riverside *Daily Press*, September 25, 1922.

8   Joan Hall, Riverside Bicentennial Place Name Map, 1976.

9   Jim Barrie, Facebook Communication, August 4, 2013.

10 Sandra Martin Maxwell, Facebook post, May 4, 2024.

11 Mary Carpenter, Facebook post, April 24, 2024.

12 Joan Hall, Riverside Bicentennial Place Name Map, 1976.

13 *Ibid.*

14 *Ibid.*

15 "Mount Rubidoux Park Unit No. 2," MB 19/99, April, 1941.

16 William St. Marie, friend of a friend who knew him and raced motorbikes near John's house, Facebook communication, August 6, 2013.

17 Joan Hall, Riverside Bicentennial Place Name Map, 1976.

18 *Ibid.*

19 Jana Cheney, Hoover house owner, Facebook post, April 24, 2024.

20 Joan Hall, Riverside Bicentennial Place Name Map, 1976.

21 *Ibid.*

22 *Ibid.*

23 *Ibid*; Joan Hall, Riverside Bicentennial Place Name Map, 1976.

24 *Ibid.*

25 *Ibid.*

26 Lorene Sisquoc, Curator of the Sherman Institute Museum, July 5, 2024.

27 Riverside *Daily Press*, October 24, 1918.

28 Jim Barrie, Facebook communication, August 4, 2013.

29 Joan Hall, Riverside Bicentennial Place Name Map, 1976.

30 Debbie Ragsdale, Facebook post, May 4, 2024.

31 Riverside *Enterprise*, February 9, 1954

32 Joan Hall, Riverside Bicentennial Place Name Map, 1976.

33 Riverside *Daily Press*, November 7, 1940.

34 Lorene Sisquoc, Curator of the Sherman Institute Museum, July 5, 2024.

35 Riverside *Press*, August 7, 1890.

36 Michael Brown, Facebook communication, April 12, 2024; Riverside *Press*, December 2, 1953.

37 Art Escalante, former Peggy Lane resident, Facebook communication, August 4, 2013.

38 Joan Hall, Riverside Bicentennial Place Name Map, 1976.

39 William Woertz III, Facebook post, April 24, 2024.

40 Riverside *Daily Press*, May 12, 1948.

41 Joan Hall, Riverside Bicentennial Place Name Map, 1976.

42 *Ibid.*

43 *Ibid.*

44 *Ibid.*

45 *Ibid.*

46 *Ibid.*

47 Robert Murphy, Facebook post, May 4, 2024.

48 Joan Hall, Riverside Bicentennial Place Name Map, 1976.

49 Caroline DeMar, Alfred and Mary Trautwein's granddaughter, personal communication with the author, June 1, 2021.

50 Bob Wilson, son of Don and Berenice Wilson, Facebook post, April 24, 2024.

51 Joan Hall, Riverside Bicentennial Place Name Map, 1976.

52 William Woertz III, Facebook post, April 24, 2024.

53 Joan Hall, Riverside Bicentennial Place Name Map, 1976.

54 Alice Gilpin-Walker, Facebook post, April 24, 2024; *Press-Enterprise*, October 24, 2019.

R 64   BUENA VISTA AVENUE AT FOOT OF MT. RUBIDOUX, WESTERN ENTRANCE TO RIVERSIDE, CALIFORNIA

2A-H136

About the Author

Steve Lech is a native Riversider who has been interested in the history of Riverside County for over 40 years. He has written or co-written 18 books on various aspects of Riverside County's history, including,

Along the Old Roads (2004) (Considered the definitive history of Riverside County);

Crocker's Folly – The Development of, and Opposition to, the Palm Springs Aerial Tramway (2023);

For Tourism and a Good Night's Sleep – J. Win Wilson, Wilson Howell, and the Beginnings of the Pines-to-Palms Highway (2012);

More Than a Place to Pitch a Tent – The Stories Behind Riverside County's Regional Parks (2011);

Back in the Day, Vols 1 - 6 (with Kim Jarrell Johnson, various dates).

In addition to writing books, he serves as editor of the Riverside County Chronicles (the Riverside County Heritage Association's journal of local history), and is on the editorial board of the Journal of the Riverside Historical Society. He is president of the Riverside Historical Society and maintains memberships in some two dozen other local historical societies throughout Riverside County and Southern California. Steve has served on and been past chair of the Riverside County Historical Commission and the City of Riverside's Cultural Heritage Board. He has been a docent with the Mission Inn Foundation in Riverside since September, 1988, is an active member of the MIF History Research Committee which seeks to document the many stories that surround Riverside's historic hotel, and has served as Director of Docent Training for the Mission Inn Foundation. Steve lives in Riverside with his wife Tracy. He retired from the County of Riverside in 2014 so he could continue to research many aspects of Riverside County's varied history.

www.ingramcontent.com/pod-product-compliance
Lightning Source LLC
LaVergne TN
LVHW012310220125
801826LV00006B/12